Little Play-a-Sound™

DAVID AND GOLIATH

Illustrated by Kelly R. Pulley

Written by Sam E. Gato

Sound designed by Kristan Nordine

Publications International, Ltd.

David's brothers went to fight the enemy of God's people. David stayed home to watch the sheep. He played his harp every day. One day, David's father asked him to take some food to his brothers in King Saul's army.

The enemy had sent their biggest and best soldier, Goliath, to fight the army of King Saul. Goliath stood almost 10 feet tall! Goliath asked for one man from Saul's army to fight against him. The men in Saul's army were afraid. They knew Goliath was very strong.

David told King Saul that he would fight the giant. "You should be guarding your sheep," said King Saul. "How can you fight Goliath?"

"God will help me," said David.

King Saul gave David a sword and armor. But the sword and the armor were too heavy for young David. Instead he chose some smooth stones from a stream. David would fight Goliath with only his sling and the stones.

David called to Goliath, "You come with a sword  and spear. But I come to you in the name of God. This battle is the Lord's." David then took one of the stones he had chosen from the stream. He put the stone into his sling.

The stone went around and around in the sling. Then it flew out and hit Goliath in the forehead. Goliath fell down with a loud thud! David trusted God, and with God's help, he won. All the people of God were glad.